Mary Engelbreit's
Outdoor Companion

Mary Engelbreit's
Outdoor Companion

The Mary Engelbreit Look and How to Get It

Illustrations by Mary Engelbreit

Written by Charlotte Lyons

Photographs by Barbara Elliott Martin

Andrews and McMeel

A Universal Press Syndicate Company

Kansas City

10 9 8 7 6 5 4 3 2

Library of Congress Cataloging-in-Publication Data

Engelbreit, Mary.
    Mary Engelbreit's outdoor companion : the Mary Engelbreit look and how to get it / illustrations by Mary Engelbreit ; written by Charlotte Lyons ; photographs by Barbara Elliott Martin.
        p.   cm.
    ISBN 0-8362-1085-9 (hc)
    1. Gardens. 2. Gardening.   3. Garden ornaments and furniture. 4. Handicraft. 5. Gardens--Pictorial works. 6. Gardening--Pictorial works. 7. Garden ornaments and furniture--Pictorial works. I. Lyons, Charlotte. II. Title.
SB455.E73   1996
712' .6--dc20   95-40322
                                                               CIP

Design by Stephanie Raaf

Contents

WOULD THAT THIS GARLAND FAIR
MIGHT WEAVE AROUND THY LIFE,
A SPELL TO SHIELD FROM CARE,
A GUARD FROM EVERY STRIFE.

ANONYMOUS

Introduction

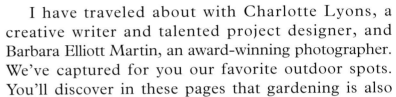I have the prettiest garden—everything grows exactly as I imagined it would. It's full of everlasting color, beautiful blooms, specimen plantings in perfect harmony. I never have to plant, weed, or wait for bloom times. And it's always right in front of me where I can enjoy it all day and evening! That's right—I drew it and colored it in with markers and pencils. In fact, I've drawn many versions of my ideal garden. I have a few invented flowers (like the ones that flower as hearts, stars, and fairies), but mostly my garden is inspired by those I have admired through the years. The ones full of luscious plantings, children playing, and birdhouses swinging in the tree— I fancy myself in every one.

Now, in truth, I'm not much of a real gardener, but over the years, I've learned a thing or two about gardening—it's as much about making a comfy spot as it is about perennials and annuals. That's what I'm really good at—making things cute and cozy. All my flea market finds take a turn outside or on the porch in the summertime. Of course, my favorites have always been birdhouses, little benches, and lots of fat pillows— whatever I can scoot around and mix with the treasures already there. In this book you'll see lots of clever ideas for porch and patio decorating, along with fun projects to help you decorate your house.

I have traveled about with Charlotte Lyons, a creative writer and talented project designer, and Barbara Elliott Martin, an award-winning photographer. We've captured for you our favorite outdoor spots. You'll discover in these pages that gardening is also about color and the way we use it outdoors in nature. There is nothing like the combination of magenta, yellow, and orange to inspire my imaginary paint-brush. Pansies, petunias, forget-me-nots, wandering ivy, and hollyhocks are some of the flowers I've grown very fond of when I draw. We were lucky enough to find some extraordinary real gardens that are full of brilliant color and creativity.

Along the way we also found sweet pet houses, fences, gates, and charming places for children. We included a chapter about bringing the outdoors in because we realized that so much of what we love seems to follow us back inside. Indeed, there's something for everyone inside these pages—whether you are a gardener, a decorator, an artist like me, or just someone who really appreciates the wonder and magic of it all.

Mary Engelbreit

For our parents—
Bob and Mary, Bob and Charlotte, George and Wanda

chapter one

"The only limit to your garden is at the boundaries of your imagination."

—Thomas D. Church

Warm weather gives the front door new importance as we linger outside—no longer rushing in and out of cold air. The entrance begins at the onset of the path leading up to the door, where we glimpse the personality of a home. Simply decorated with pots of posies on either side, or elaborately expressed with hand-painted detail, welcoming benches, and exuberant plantings, your doorway says hello to each visitor long before she reaches for the bell.

We like entrances that give a hint about the spirit of the house. If you are a gardener, plant the way. An artist might decorate the door with paint and imagination. Give yourself and your guests a place to sit and watch the world pass by or a secluded spot where you can retreat to be alone. Even a bench tucked along the walk is an invitation to stop and visit. Meandering pathways to other garden areas can be inviting in themselves. A formal path to the front door can become a garden trimmed with blooming borders. In winter, everyone will scurry past again. For now, welcome your family, friends, and, of course, yourself with a heartfelt greeting that says "I'm so glad you're here."

Perfect symmetry and formality are relaxed here when pale pink flowers, delicate wire benches, and the fanciful cutout butler holding a pot at the door are added to the scene (opposite). The corkscrew topiaries are softened by geraniums and ivy tumbling out of concrete urns.

The island in the driveway
seems the perfect place for this favorite birdhouse
perched high above the garden (below).
All around it, petunias, kale, and little daisies cushion the earth.
The back door porch nicely accommodates the vintage sign,
although Rosie much prefers the outdoor summer breezes.

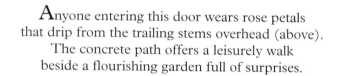

Anyone entering this door wears rose petals
that drip from the trailing stems overhead (above).
The concrete path offers a leisurely walk
beside a flourishing garden full of surprises.

Abundantly in bloom, a backyard cutting garden marches right up to the doorway,
lending picturesque exuberance to the neutral colors of this handsome house.

An enchanting Comstock cottage sparkles like a fairy tale at the top of a stony path.
Old-fashioned flowers meander through ferns and shrubbery
as vines trail around the door of Sunrise Turn Cottage.

Cattails and a tropical crane animate a vintage screen door
of a southern cottage (below).
Fresh paint and strong sunlight give the doorway
an inviting impact.

A kitchen screen door in a courtyard
catches morning sunlight and birdsong (above).
The bench and twig planter are welcoming furnishings
that are easy to care for in a mostly green space.

A courtyard garden offers entry through a gabled doorway
designed to repeat the architecture of the house tucked behind the wall (below).
The heavy wooden door and rough, clay walls give a mysterious,
old-world feeling that is intriguing, though decidedly private.

The niche surrounding these double doors
provides a sheltered spot
perfect for a bench (opposite).
Pots of trailing ivy cascade on the wall
and mix easily
with movable containers of easy-care annuals.

Here's a front yard happily given to bloom. Even the chimney is drenched in ivy.
How wonderful to always come and go through a garden!

Over Mary's screen porch door,
two Scotties enliven a transom (below).
Cut with a jigsaw and backed with screen,
they add just the right touch to a summery retreat.

In a city church garden,
a beguiling arbor of potato vine
beckons shopping villagers and churchgoers
to take the corner shortcut that twists through
a well-loved perennial garden (above).

A vast brick entry is embedded
with boxwood hedges set into planters (below).
At Christmastime the owner places
a Christmas tree in each spot.
Visitors are greeted by a forest of white lights and evergreens.

Running down the middle of a driveway
that also acts as a garden path,
lush ground cover breaks the expanse of brick
into twin walks alongside a vegetable garden (above).
The doors are built in the spirit of barn doors,
further relaxing the garage effect.

Once an old grocery store
and now an artist's studio residence,
this doorway opens right onto
a sun-drenched sidewalk,
leaving little room for decoration.
The striking yellow door
was painted by the artist
to give permanent vitality to the entrance
and to announce a creative spirit within.
It is complemented by the totem pole
and small chairs that act as plant stands.

With imagination and brush,
a stack of painted clay pots lights the way
to the back door (below).

A Victorian screen door emphatically demonstrates
the owner's ardent preference for purple (above).
Set amid the wall of detailed shingles,
it becomes a natural focal point.
Painting the shingles before they were installed
made the finish work easier—
although even this required an artist's brush.

Gardener's Workbench

Birdbath

Materials:

- 3 clay pots that nest in increasing sizes: 12", 14", 16"
- 1 clay saucer 20" in diameter or at least 4" larger than the largest clay pot
- Acrylic paints in assorted colors
- Brushes
- Acrylic sealer
- Construction glue and caulking gun

How To:

Begin with the largest pot turned over and stack the clay pots upside down to see how they will fit together before painting. Mark where they overlap to be sure the decoration won't be hidden by the pots when they are stacked.

Base paint each pot and the saucer in the colors of your choice. Paint inside the rim too. Add decorative patterns shown here or as you wish.

When dry, seal all painted and unpainted areas with acrylic sealer—especially the inside of the saucer. Stack and use construction glue to fortify the joints. Then use the glue to affix the saucer right-side up to the stacked pots.

Fill with water.

"You don't have a garden just for yourself.
You have it to share."

—Augusta Carter

chapter two

GATEWAYS

"Nature does not complete things. She is chaotic.
Man must finish, and he does so by making a garden and building a wall."

—Robert Frost

Coming in and out of the garden creates opportunities to continually delight in the gardener's efforts. Gateways, whether they are elaborately fashioned from wrought iron or simple bowers where a birdhouse swings over a pathway, encourage the visitor to slow her step and consider the enthralling spectacle of a garden. The airy canopy of an arbor is a romantic flourish—a nostalgic reminder of old-fashioned gardens. When it connects to a fence, an arbor is an inviting passage to a comforting enclosure.

Fences are used for different reasons, which include essential privacy as well as overall garden definition. Even a plain lawn looks more appealing when surrounded by an attractive fence, whether it's a rickety picket fence where stray blooms peek through the slats or a newer one decorated with cutouts and clever trims. Remember that any outdoor decoration should complement the general architecture and style of the house and the artistry of the garden.

■ ■ ■ ■ ■ ■

Mary's arbor gate is especially charming with
the unique design of a cutout pot and bloom (opposite).
The overhead pergola holds planter boxes
in which she can rotate seasonal annuals
to provide sunny bands of color.

Cutouts in a repeat pattern
decorate an architectural fence at the beach (below).
The rolling waves and starfish
add charm to an otherwise plain fence.

An older picket fence among foxgloves and delphinium
weaves its way through a ranch garden (left).
Within the large garden, the fence creates small spaces
adorned with vintage birdhouses and theme plantings.

A little planter full of blooms sweetens a picket gate leading the way to a courtyard garden where a kitty house stands near the door. These little touches give the most heart to a garden.

This arbor gate cloaked in rambling grapevines is a romantic passage from one garden to the next.
The clock birdhouse reminds us that time flies when you're having fun—especially in this transcendent garden.

A tiny city lot enclosed by an old-fashioned picket fence
boasts a storybook entrance.
The sun-swept view of the shingled cottage and cutout shutters beyond
is irresistible to visitors who stop to revel in the charm.

An arbor at the edge of the woods
shelters a rustic resting spot (below).
A table for lemonade and tired feet
is all that is needed—there is peace and quiet too.

Porch windows are rimmed in arbors
where roses ramble right up to the screens (above).
The fragrance filters through to the porch
while bees buzz harmlessly outside.

A moon gate stands sentinel across a brick pathway where visitors pause
to consider the pretty gardens just traveled and still beyond.
The side supports provide a climbing post for summer clematis, aglow with crimson blooms.

A waist-high lattice fence and brick pavers
carve a little garden patio out of a side yard (opposite).
Flea-market chairs and narrow flower beds
make the most of the shady nook.
Odd wooden ornaments take their places here and there,
adding to the casual charm.

So close to the street, this sweet cottage protects its privacy
with a gate designed to attract attention,
but keep passersby at bay (above).
The little gate box often holds messages from friends
who can't resist its tiny door and curious carved bear.

Protected by a brick wall, this courtyard
has a bewitching secret garden feeling (above).
The painted wooden gate curtained by a tangle of vines
lends a distinctly Old English flavor
to this very private garden.

The corner of an elevated deck and its spectacular view provided the beginning for this gazebo (left). Lattice enclosure and bench seating at the table give the feeling of being in a treehouse.

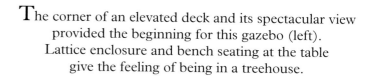

Trellised ivy weaves an artful pattern against a plain wall (above). Guidelines of string or wire form the pattern base. Careful pruning, the kind necessary for a topiary, keeps it uniform.

Sidewalk entrance gates swing open beneath an arbor
that repeats the design of the breezeway gazebo
full of wicker chairs (above and right).
The space between holds a compact garden
surrounding the fountain.

A shady oasis
seems like just the right spot
for this pastoral scene
built into an iron gate (left).
It is one of many reminders
that this tranquil garden sanctuary
is for the contemplative wanderer.

Wrought iron angels and topiary baskets
decorate driveway gates
that are right in keeping with the style of the house—
elegant and lovely (right).

Gardener's Workbench

Wind Chime

Materials:

- Tin sand pail
- 5 or 6 sand shovels
- Fishing line of a sturdy weight
- Hammer and large nail
- 2" x 4" wood scrap as long or longer than the depth of the pail

How To:

Turn the sand pail upside down and, with a pencil, mark 5 or 6 places for holes that would evenly distribute the shovels as they hung from the bottom of the pail. Insert the 2" x 4" wood scrap into it so that it fits against the inside bottom of the pail.

With the wood scrap inside, place the nail on a marked hole and use the hammer to strike the nail and pierce the pail. Do this for all the holes you have marked. Thread twenty-inch strands of fishing line through each of the shovel handles and tie securely.

Experiment with hanging lengths that suit the look and sound of the shovels clanging against each other and then thread the free ends through the holes in the bottom of the pail. Adjust the lengths and tie them to the nail securely. Drop the nail back into the sand pail with all the lines attached to it. Hang the pail from its handle and adjust again as necessary.

"One should learn also to enjoy the neighbor's garden, however small;
the roses straggling over the fence,
the scent of lilacs drifting across the road."

—Henry Van Dyke

WHO LOVES A GARDEN STILL HIS EDEN KEEPS

A.B. ALCOTT

chapter three

BLOOMERS

"Show me your garden and I shall tell you what you are."

—Alfred, Lord Tennyson

There are as many different kinds of gardens as there are people to invent them. City gardens that are confined to movable pots are cherished equally, along with acres of botanical delights.

Perhaps most important is the vision of the gardener, and the implementation of that vision. Consider first your time and resources available for the garden: Is this where you wish to spend long summer hours planting, nurturing, cutting, and creating, or do you just want a lush outdoor room for reading and dining? Always be guided by what you consider enjoyable and don't create another chore when it could be a delightful hobby.

Whatever you choose, the natural environment will dictate many of the choices yet to be made. A simple sundial in a tiny courtyard is all that might be needed to inspire a tranquil garden spot. Add a weatherworn bench and suddenly, it's an alluring garden retreat where an unplanned pathway finds its end, where children come to play hide-and-seek, and where you escape to consider other projects yet to come.

An artist's studio door opens to a terrace awash with an overflowing profusion of blossoms (opposite). The flurry of dazzling color offers refreshment and inspiration whenever the painter leaves her canvas for the magnificent view.

This enclosed kitchen garden
teeming with bushy vegetables
sits in the midst of a wide lawn (below).
The fence and leafy shrubs behind it frame it effectively.
An aisle of flagstone is all the cook needs to tend,
cultivate, and harvest each planting.

Roses and delphinium nod their heads to an ancient birdhouse
that is set low enough to be more of an ornament
than an apartment (above).

A garden border is reflected above in the window box arrangement.
Even the ornamental signs reappear at the window. The wooden birds add color and whimsy to this wild-looking spot.

A four-square inside a classic white fence is centered around a sundial.
Herbs and vegetables are forced to behave themselves inside this formal arrangement.
The varied shades of green are as interesting as bands of colored blossoms.

Simple planter boxes are anything but
when they're sparked with finials and flowers (below).
Tightly planted with herbs and annuals
such as pansies, dusty miller, and spearmint,
they are a perfect foil to the carefully mowed lawn
surrounding them.

A slip of a space by the back door
gives room enough for a thriving vegetable plot (above).
Tightly packed with zinnias, corn, and tomatoes,
it serves the homeowner well.

Mary's backyard pond
is the best spot to wile away
summer afternoons
with her sons (opposite).
Toy boats skitter across the water,
bubbles dance through the air,
and goldfish shimmer beneath lily pads.
Mary's sketch pad
records it all in doodles
of lazy summer fun
that are excellent inspiration
for drawings still to come.

Clouds of purple violas and Johnny-jump-ups encircle a platter fountain
in the center of a courtyard (above).
Staying with a color scheme—here based on purple—
creates order in a diverse planting area.

A slice of heaven waits here where a dainty perennial bed cozies up to a gracious lawn chair.
The wand of tall grasses builds an unobtrusive backdrop for the bloomers, yet leads the eye beyond to the lake.
Redwing blackbirds trill their summer song from whispering cattails at the shore.

The front yard of this town cottage
has been completely surrendered to the medley of flowers
planted in the place of grass (below).
The gardener accepted the challenge
to plant the brightest varieties she could find—
and as many of them as she could fit!

A window box garden tumbles over
with a profusion of trailing geranium (above).
Watering from the open window is all that it needs.

Plant stakes mimic tree trunks lined up against the brick wall
in a city garden that still has room
for vegetables and perennials (below).
Knowing what you value in a garden makes the happiest plan.

Predominantly green and white plantings
create natural coolness in a Texas garden (right).
The earthy path contributes to the forestlike feeling
while offering a direct route to another garden room beyond.

Stepping stones and a rough-cut, staked border outline a shortcut from one garden to another. Rustic garden ornaments and taller hedges promise more surprises yet to be encountered.

Nasturtiums thrive
near a summer reflecting pool
beside a pergola walkway
that trims the garden (opposite).

A formal patio water garden successfully blends plant material and architecture
in many sculptural shapes (above).
The rough-cut chairs play against the glassy water surface,
the boulders counterpoint the lattice fence,
and the shooting stalks of iris complement the trimmed topiary orb.
Neutral colors unify the group and create an environment
that is easy on the eye and the senses.

A very narrow brick pathway insists that visitors and caretakers proceed slowly.
Specimen plantings are meant to be enjoyed both alone and together with those that crowd in beside them.
The tiny patio at the end of the path is just big enough for two twiggy chairs and a glorious view.

A stone foundation wall is a classic backdrop
for an herb garden carefully laid out
in a bed of bark chips (below).
The winding stone path and raised edge
draw the eye to the various plantings.
The straw bee skep is a traditional herb garden ornament.

A bungalow veiled in creeping ivy opens its windows
to boxes of purple and white annuals (above).
Cleome edges the walk and interrupts the greenness
with explosive bursts of magenta.

A dramatic fountain bubbles beneath an iron grate bridge that connects the multilevel deck to the historic house. Rugged brick is studded with craggy plantings and the handrail is fortified by bountiful pots of bloom. The mix of old and new creates a stunning urban garden.

A Stonehenge bridge makes this gazebo retreat
a magical getaway (below).
Lilies and hostas are low maintenance
but dramatic choices for plantings.

A swimming pool and hot tub,
surrounded by flagstone and ever-blooming annuals,
blend naturally into the garden (left).

A vast and rambling vegetable garden
can become a visual feast
with the addition of sculptural art scarecrows
and architectural birdhouses (above and right).

The entrance to this back yard is a simple arbor that mimics the style of the buildings nearby. Climbing roses dress it up and create a welcoming focal point.

Pan and his flutes stand watch
over an herb garden in its infancy (below).
Even something as simple as lettuce offers interest
because of the myriad color variations of the leaves.

Rectangular flower beds edged with stone
make the most of a spot of sunshine near the house (above).
Tightly planted with brilliant blooms,
they create scattered pockets of color among
steadfast green shrubbery.

Gardener's Workbench

Cherries Bucket

Materials:
- Metal garden pail or bucket
- Black spray paint
- Acrylic paints in red, green, and white
- Brushes
- Acrylic sealer
- Newspaper and masking tape

How To:

Mask off the handle, and its attachments to the bucket, with newspaper and tape. Turn the bucket upside down and spray paint it black on the outside only. When dry, paint a band of green beneath the rim.

When it's dry, paint white squares below the band to make a checkerboard. Randomly scatter single red cherries and clusters all over the rest of the bucket. Add stems and leaves going in different directions so that it creates an encircling pattern. Use the tip of a fine brush to drop dots of white paint randomly across the remaining black spaces.

When dry, seal with acrylic sealer.

■ ■ ■ ■ ■ ■

"Heaven is under our feet as well as over our heads."
—Henry David Thoreau

BLOOM WHERE YOU'RE PLANTED

chapter four

HERE and THERE

"But a little garden, the littler the better,
is your richest chance of happiness and success."

—Reginald Farrer

Always on the lookout for more places for plants, gardeners and outdoor decorators find lots of opportunities in window boxes and container gardens. Containers and window boxes are easy to take care of, provide an extra punch of color, and allow us to bring plants to new situations. Anything goes as long as it has drainage and the right mix of plants for the container. Old boots bursting with bloom will bring a smile to any garden. A basket of moss and ferns adds interest to a shady corner. Painted pots, cracked dishes—anything you want to surrender to the dirt and watering—will be the beginning of a movable garden.

Aside from attached window boxes (which can be dressed up with cutouts or paint), pots and planters are easy to scoot around into the sunlight, or to rotate for a better face. Grouping several in different heights and shapes will give the feeling of a whole garden; just one will draw attention to the furnishings nearby. Try hanging an old chair on a board fence for an unusual pot holder or filling an old wagon with a cushion of blossoms. It certainly gives you something to talk about when you walk a visitor through the garden.

The enchantment of this storybook look
comes from the contrast of the brightly colored blooms
against the dappled building (opposite).
Tumbling foliage falls from pots
sitting on a plank shelf built into the house.
The rail fence and lanky perennials
provide the perfect complement.

Painted clay pots with bright polka dots
perch on a quaint shelf (opposite).
They seem right at home with hand-painted birdhouses
clustered on the rustic fence.

A wooden farm cart provides a raised focal point
for assorted pots of annuals (above).
In a driveway, this movable garden breaks up the space
with color and foliage.

A New England–style shingled cottage stands
as a cozy backdrop for a battalion of potted flowers (above).
Planted in this way,
pots can be rotated for best sunlight and blooms.

A toddler's red wagon packed with summer annuals becomes a portable garden.
Drainage holes punched through the bottom before planting allow the shallow garden to take frequent waterings and to drain freely.

Mexican chairs for children
take a turn as pot holders
for pansies on a handmade fence (below).
The intricate grate and handmade trim
help build a fanciful garden corner
beneath wandering wisteria vines.
The garden easily inspires reveries of faraway places.

Charlotte's playhouse window
box mixes annuals with perennials for vivid color play (above).
The box itself is decorated with a painted-on scalloped trim
and a bouquet of year-round posies.
In the fall, she plants the perennials in the ground
for next summer's flowers.

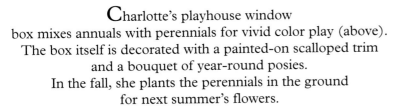

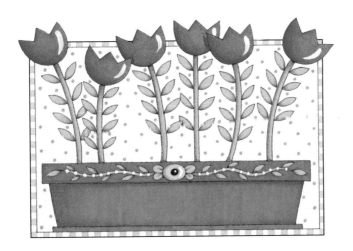

A fancy-cut apron makes a simple window box
a showstopper (below).
This could be cut from plywood
and attached to any window box for some pizzazz.

Gray stucco walls amplify the brilliant plant colors that
contrast with the bright white trim and royal blue shutters (above).
A weatherworn park bench adds another element of texture
and comfort to a scene that could transport the visitor
to another continent.

An unbelievable array of blooms brightens a stone courtyard (left).

In a perennial border, a big bucket of geraniums is suspended from an iron stake (above). Like a birdhouse, it draws the eye upward and creates interest above the garden.

A Michigan cottage uses easy-care petunias to brighten window boxes (left). Pinching them back on weekend visits ensures lush summer growth.

Gardener's Workbench

Planter Box

Materials:

- A planter box or suitable substitute such as a wooden wine crate
- Decorative trim for edges of your box
- 4 ball-shaped curtain rod ends
- 1/4" luan plywood for cutouts or craft store cutouts in shapes of your choice
- Jigsaw and wood glue for cutout method
- Drill
- Acrylic paints
- Brushes
- Acrylic sealer

How To:

Drill drainage holes into the bottom of the box. Add trim to the edges of the box as desired. Screw the curtain rod ends into the bottom for feet. Paint the box white.

Refering to the photograph, draw pattern shapes onto some newspaper. Cut out the pattern shapes and use them as templates: either cut out the shapes from the plywood or trace them onto the box so that you can paint them onto the sides. Paint as shown in photograph. Apply the cutouts with wood glue if you have made them.

When dry, apply sealer over the entire piece to weatherproof it.

"A morning glory at my window
satisfies me more than the metaphysics of books."

—Walt Whitman

chapter five

FORGET·ME·NOTS

"Summer afternoon–summer afternoon; to me those have always been
the two most beautiful words in the English language."

—Henry James

The outdoors is enjoyed the most when it offers a place to sit and relax in its midst. This could be a patio drenched in sunlight or shade; it could be an enclosed screened porch that has the feeling of being both indoors and out.

Cozying up a porch with lovely fabrics, pots of plants, books, and collectibles is a favorite spring activity. Furnishings that can take the weather changes and provide carefree comfort are best. Collectibles like birdhouses, garden ornaments, and pottery fit in easily, as do easy-care rugs or mats underfoot. Use old china pitchers and teapots for fresh-cut flowers. Also, consider baskets and hampers for magazines and books or toys and games that everyone enjoys.

Whenever possible, make room for casual dining outdoors too. Trays or tables that move about will work here, as will a more formal eating area set with table and chairs. Lamp- or candlelight is captivating in the evening and encourages guests to linger in the friendly darkness long after the meal is finished. This is a wonderful place for relaxing with family and friends—or even alone. So make the most of your outdoor room with individual touches that make it your own.

EVERYONE NEEDS THEIR OWN SPOT.

·ROBERT WHALEN·

Here is a charming table
made from an old martin house (opposite).
Simple slatted chairs are a perfect match
on this patio near the kitchen.

An open porch walk is finished off
with a pair of chairs where the gardener
can admire the results of her hard work (below).

Copied from Leo Tolstoy's historic Russian home,
these slat cutouts work their magic
on an American porch (above).
Vintage linens on pillows and a child's rocker
complete the charming scene.

Lunch is served on a woodland patio table where shady trees keep this outdoor room cool and pleasant (right).

Sunshine spotlights a deck and garden.
A solitary chaise invites one to linger
in the sun (above).

Every summer
Charlotte and Andy's front porch
becomes the favorite living area
(opposite).
Furnished with a rag rug,
toys, and board games,
it becomes an outdoor family room
where children gather
with neighborhood playmates
and grown-ups relax
in the dusky twilight after supper.

A gorgeous pergola checkers the deck with squares of sunlight (above).
Petunias thrive in the brightness beneath the open canopy.

Lamplight and pictures on the wall
warm a porch corner (opposite).
Try bringing some well-loved pieces from other rooms
out into the sunshine for a season.
They look so different in new places.

A walk-through screened porch
leads the way to a shady garden outside (above).

Nothing could be more inviting
than a screened porch full of good books, downy pillows,
and summer breezes (above).
Mary has it all carefully collected on her porch
outside her summer studio.
Old rattan furniture, striped cushions, and favorite curios
make a cozy refuge that the whole family enjoys.

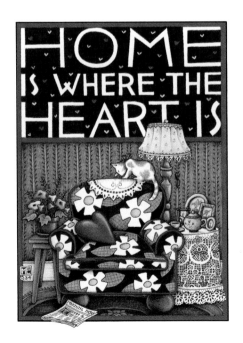

A garage wall covered in ivy creates an enticing backdrop
for a seating area in a townhouse garden (left).
Pots of flowers and iron furniture plumped with cushions
furnish the shady retreat.
The blue and white china pitcher full of peonies
adds color and thoughtfulness.
Tea is on its way.

Right outside the bedroom
a private patio shelters a romantic breakfast spot
just big enough for two (above).

Two old cedar chairs take a well-deserved sunbath in a cozy corner of a carefully overgrown garden (below).

Just for the day—when you're sure it will not rain—
take a pretty rug out into the garden,
along with a bunch of festive pillows (above).
Comfort is always worth the trouble.

Sandy shoes happily wait on the porch sweetened with pink porch rockers and favorite finds.
The bear holds a bouquet of farmer's market flowers which tells the visitor everything she needs to know
about the welcome offered here—it's fresh and friendly. Count on it!

A back porch seating area is the perfect place
to dream up a summer menu (below).
The painted-on rug and potful of garden picks
make it comfy and sweet.
It's hard to get up and head back to the kitchen.

A slim slip of a corner offers vertical interest
with an arrangement of antique reinforcing stars
and sprightly topiaries on a weathered worktable (above).
The terra cotta pots and the brick
link all the elements into one unified arrangement.

All set for summer, this porch sparkles with cheerful shades of indigo and rose.
Vintage linens are fun to collect and use for decorating—their years of use add to the casual mood.

Gardener's Workbench

Painted Deck Chair

Materials:
- Folding deck chair
- Removable canvas seat and back
- Acrylic paints
- Brushes
- Permanent marker

How To:

Paint large patterned flowers here and there across the seat. Add leaf shapes in varying combinations and directions.

On the back of the chair, mark three panels in proportions similar to what is pictured here. Paint the two outside panels green. With the permanent marker, write out one of your favorite gardening quotes. You may want to do this first in pencil in case of errors. In the center panel, paint a favorite flower design.

Scatter white dots over all.

"The main purpose of a garden
is to give its owner the best and highest kind of earthly pleasure."

—Gertrude Jekyll

THE SIMPLE NEWS
THAT NATURE TOLD,
WITH TENDER MAJESTY

EMILY DICKINSON

chapter six

UNDER the APPLE TREE

"How do you like to go up in a swing?
Up in the air so blue?
Oh, I do think it is the pleasantest thing
Ever a child can do!"

—Robert Louis Stevenson

Sharing a garden with children infinitely increases the enjoyment of an outdoor space. The sound of laughter and children's voices easily rivals birdsong as one of a gardener's treasured rewards. Secret hideaways, places to play, and plants to tend are sweet enticements that delight young and old.

Creating special areas in the garden for children is wonderfully rewarding and brings magic to any yard. Playhouses are the most obvious choice here: they not only give a child a special place, but they give the builder a fabulous project based on imagination and loving indulgence. It's a chance to recapture the pleasure of our childhood fantasies. A little structure of this kind becomes a visual highlight in the garden and gives added charm to everything surrounding it.

You might consider a special seating area with child-sized chairs and toys, or a vegetable plot for children that encourages them to feel a part of the garden. Invite them to help you with the tasks and thrills of gardening—they become experts very quickly and their companionship is invaluable.

■ ■ ■ ■ ■ ■

MAKE A NEST of PLEASANT THOUGHTS.

JOHN RUSKIN

A plain canvas tepee is transformed by a painter's whimsy and imagination (opposite).
What a fantastic portable playhouse!

No detail was overlooked in the design of this flamboyant playhouse.
This little piggy mailbox stashes all kinds of messages and giggles.

It even has a faux fireplace
providing year-round coziness (below)!

The floor was painted
to replicate grandma's linoleum of long ago (above).

While the shingles are extravagant,
the curly slide is our favorite feature (left).

97

Tucked against the garden wall is a dwelling fit for a dreamy fairytale.
The wandering vines add mystery to the refuge.

An impromptu tea party in the garden
delivers all the fun of a real one
when fluffy cushions and fancy hats come into play (below).

A garden with children in mind
has several inviting spots of whimsy (above).
Having their own spot in a garden gives children a chance
to tend vegetables and flowers that they grow themselves.
Herbs are especially fine for this as they can be picked frequently
and proudly brought to the table.

Rabbit Cottage is a popular retreat for Charlotte's girls,
where they love to cook with rocks and sand (below).
Lace curtains fill windows without glass,
giving the feeling of home.
Painted-on trim adds more quick-and-easy adornment.

Children can't resist picking flowers
in a garden (above).
A paper cup in a basket hung on a fence
makes a small posyholder perfect for a handful.

An ME-style playhouse
pops up in a fenced yard (right).
It distinguishes itself with sunflower accents
and bright green paint trim.
The builder made two of these houses simultaneously
and donated one to a children's charity auction.

At the back of a shady yard,
a new playhouse elicits nostalgia for the charm of yesteryear
with the help of vintage windows and an older door (right).
The shady hideaway inspires pretend games
throughout the summer.

This playhouse belonged to the owner
when she was a little girl (above).
Brought from home like any other treasure,
it now gives her children a special memory too.

A field trip to a meadow of wildflowers
becomes a natural playground
for exploration and adventure (right).

Bright paint colors and creative design
enliven a playground corner where a simple seesaw becomes
art sculpture (below).

A decorated chair stashed under the pines invites children
to play, read, and study nature (above).

Gardener's Workbench

Gardening Tote

Materials:

- Unfinished wooden crafter's tote
- Paper cutouts and labels
- Mod Podge®, wallpaper paste, or thin glue
- Acrylic paints
- Brushes
- Acrylic sealer

How To:

Paint the tote inside and out with black paint. Repeat with a second coat if needed. Use the paste of your choice to glue on paper cutouts where you like. Be sure they are firmly in place and that all edges are glued. Remove any excess glue from painted background.

Use the side of a 1/2"-wide artist's brush to decorate the rim with a painted checkered design. Use a fine-tipped brush to paint the handle with a trailing vine and leaves.

When dry, apply acrylic sealer over the entire piece.

"Joys divided are increased."

—Josiah Gilbert Holland

chapter seven

YARDWORK

"Nothing's beautiful from every point of view."

—Horace

The business of gardening and outdoor living involves a ceaseless amount of work and organization. Toolsheds and other outbuildings can be dressed up like any other part of the house, bringing them into the overall plan. Vintage garden tools and ornaments, such as old birdhouses and statuary, can visually transform a work area into a lovely setting. Look for unusual finds to try in the garden—a wooden cutout sign, a sculptural rake, stacks of weathered clay pots, or an interesting bench. Mix and match these elements until a decor develops that softens the scene.

Take advantage of fencing and build privacy screens for work areas if you can't improve them with decoration. Pet buildings are rewarding and creative projects. Show your affection for your dog by building a whimsical house that suits your pet's needs and your decorating instincts. From painted-on trompe l'oeil curtains in a garage to a bungalow for cats, the possibilities stretch as far as the imagination.

THE GREAT END OF LIFE IS NOT KNOWLEDGE BUT ACTION.
THOMAS HENRY HUXLEY

Way back in a corner of the yard,
a little nook cloaks a worktable wrapped in lattice (opposite).
Tools, pots, cuttings, and seeds keep close company
with mature plants.
Project ideas and notes are tacked to the wall
of a weatherproof shed door for quick reference and inspiration.

Draped with wisteria, a workshed has an alluring appeal
enhanced by grandmother's strawhat,
pots of summer-worn annuals, and a wood rake
put to the test as a rack for drying blooms (opposite).

A chair of bowlies spills over next to fully blooming containers of
geraniums and petunias (above).
The no-fuss mix of clay, wood, and old paint
contrasts effectively with the formality of brick steps.

The martin house stands too low for birds,
but makes a clever spot for a garden hose
hung on an old porch post (above).

A kitchen patio features an elaborate haven built for pet doves.
A screened porch and enclosed room keep them safe and comfortable, but near enough that their sweet cooing can be heard indoors.

Pampered chickens roost snugly in a cottage
made just for them (below).
From a shady suburban yard,
they lend rural charm
and cackles to an otherwise quiet lane.

Buttons and Bows are the cherished rabbits
that live in this shuttered hutch (above).
The area beneath the elevated apartment
keeps essential pet care items out of sight.
Children and the family cat
frequently follow the pavestone path to visit the pair.

A collection of watering cans
drips from fence pickets lining the driveway (left).
Set among movable pots,
they wait to be put to work and filled in turn.

Lushly flowering plants at the nursery
are enough to inspire any gardening plan (right).
Mick, the gardener's dog,
watches from the truck's window.
The rails have been peppered
with lucky charms cut with a jigsaw.

Although the wall hides a utilitarian service area,
it puts its best face forward with a collection of stone orbs, spare pots, and container plants.
Working diagonally, from the top corner of the wall to the opposite corner near the ground,
visually links one arrangement to the other without overdoing it.

Layered wood cutouts and paint
transform an ordinary mailbox
into a whimsical landmark (below).

A garage built with a steeply pitched roof
has room now for a second floor office-studio (above).
Cupola, shutters, and window boxes fool the eye
and dress up a plain jane utility building into an inviting retreat.

T his house is built into a hill,
and the chimney is eye level with the road (below).
What a visual surprise it provides with a nest built of sticks
and a family of storks atop the tower.

A hefty dinner bell
leads the eye to a hose rack
fashioned from painted steel (above).
The rabbit silhouette
reveals the owner's love of small animals.

Rosie is definitely living the dog's life
in a house of her own,
with dog-bone shutters, a window box,
and T-bone steaks for porch supports (opposite).

Beginning with a simple workbench against an old fence,
interest is stimulated by the folksy sign resting on top
and the rough texture of the firewood stacked
in the space beneath (below).
Contrasting the decorative elements with the functional
allows this work area to be a spirited part of the garden scheme.

This kitty bungalow is an architectural wonder of imagination,
color, and affection (above).
Three cats share its shelter
and the roof makes an excellent sun porch perch.

A sandy walk sorts its way casually
along the back of beach houses (below).
Pretty fences trim the path and add to the privacy
of both homeowners and passersby.

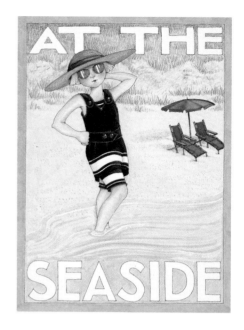

Mary's beach house garage
had a little window begging for curtains (right).
Paint and brush worked faster than fabric and thread
to make faux lace panels.
Best of all, there's nothing to wash and iron.
A few real decorations on the sill are just the right finish.

Gardener's Workbench

Garden Jacket

Materials:

- Two vintage tablecloths in bright colors and patterns
- Buttons in whatever colors you like
- Sewing pattern for a loose fitting jacket
- Sewing machine
- Thread, pins, scissors

How To:

Wash, iron, and lay out both tablecloths to choose the best aspects of their designs and patterns (try to avoid stubborn stains altogether, or place them at the seams, where they won't be noticed.) Pin and cut one cloth according to the sewing pattern requirements.

Use the second cloth for sleeves, pockets, and facings as you wish. Be sure to include roomy patch pockets even if your pattern doesn't feature them. Sew according to the pattern instructions. Use big red buttons, or another color if you prefer.

If you are making this as a gift, fill the pockets with seed packets and garden tools.

"Every garden is a chore sometimes,
but no real garden is nothing but a chore."

—Nancy Grasby

TO KNOW IS NOTHING AT ALL; TO IMAGINE IS EVERYTHING.

ANATOLE FRANCE THIBAULT

chapter eight

OUTSIDE-IN

"Arranging a bowl of flowers in the morning can give a sense of quiet in a crowded day—
like writing a poem or saying a prayer."

—Anne Morrow Lindbergh

It's certainly no accident that most decorative pieces have flowers as their central design. Bringing the outdoors back inside with us is an irresistible urge born of our love for color, nature, and warmth. Dried flowers suspended from the living room ceiling add color and fragrance for a day spent indoors. An armload of cut field stems carries the mystery of the garden into the night in a kitchen where guests will share dinner. Posy holders filled with the smallest clusters of everyday blossoms draw our attention to their new-found sweetness.

Sunny patterns created on fabrics, china, and furnishings allow us to keep the memory of summer with us year-round. Weaving these textiles into our daily lives keeps our homes cheerful and homey.

In winter, lots of brightly colored linens stacked on a kitchen shelf can have the same effect as a bouquet of daisies. Paint used on canvas, furniture, or walls enhances a room with outdoor images powerful enough to boost our spirits in any season. Experiment with your favorite ways of bringing the outdoors indoors and keep your home alive with the warmth of summer.

In a delightful summer cottage,
the garden continues inside on vintage towels and dishes (opposite).
The cookie jar full of gladiolas meets its match
in the vibrantly colored accessories.

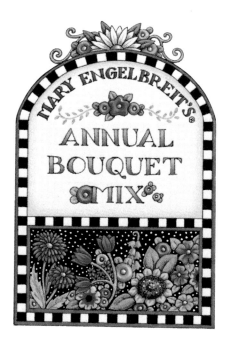

Vintage seed packets ring the opening
of a kitchen doorway with charm
and summery spirit (left, and below).
The brilliant blue walls beyond
are a sumptuous backdrop
for this harvest of color
bordered with crisp white trim.

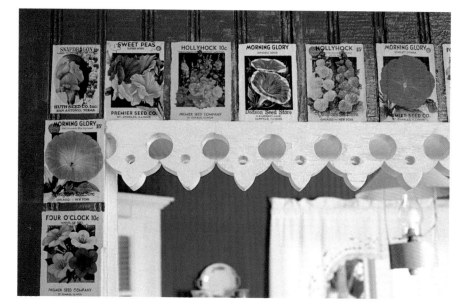

Wildflowers and lilies
fill a pottery vase
with the bounty of summer (below).
Set beside a tray of color-washed vegetables,
the savory pleasures of the season
enhance the evening meal.

Fireplaces in summer beg to be cooled
with fresh decorating (above).
On the mantel, blue candles look like spikes of veronica
beside a bowl full of zinnias and daisies.
The tower of sparkling glass cakeplates
further adds to the summery feeling.

Inside or out?
This breezeway softens the transition
from one to the other
with creeping ivy trailing everywhere (opposite).
The ceiling papered in matchstick blinds
adds texture and a climbing surface.

A cozy breakfast room employs an antique spice bin
as a window box (above).
Dried arrangements keep company with houseplants
to make the room welcoming in any season.

Outside, the greenery traces summer curtains
of lacy sunlight and translucent leaves
against the windows (above).
Inside, a wreath made from last summer's blossoms
stands as a tribute to everlasting loveliness.

A collection of thrift shop posy holders
gathers on a sunny bedroom windowsill (below).
Although perfectly adorable alone,
they are much more fun
when packed with garden blooms and clustered together.
This would be a sweet welcoming touch for a houseguest.

Fabrics full of nostalgic charm
evoke the garden outside (above).
The painting is the perfect companion to the hat stand—
both do their best to keep the garden in mind
long after it disappears in winter.

Closet doors decorated with handpainted topiaries
flank a guest room reading table (below).

The muted patina of old florals
found on china and fabrics
is enhanced by a valance of tiles trimming the fireplace (above).
The wire shelf has a window box feeling
when filled with stems of ivy trailing from an old pitcher.
No matter the season,
this room manages to feel like summer all year.

A kitchen window sprigged with herbs and flowers
is brightened year-round with the clear and cheerful color
of the tilework (opposite).
Yellow sunflowers and citrus vividly punctuate the room
with a blast of fresh sunshine.

The ceiling in Mary's sun room
was painted to replicate a glass conservatory
and the view beyond,
which includes her son in an amazing flying machine (above).

A windowsill is home
to an indoor garden vignette (above).

Funky garden whirligigs and crafters ornaments take their places in a home office (right).

A summer harvest carries its colorful promise into winter with blooms drying from the ceiling waiting to be woven into wreaths (below).

Kids' cowboy boots rustle with cactus planted right inside (above). Look around you for unusual containers that can endure the whimsy of indoor gardening.

Gardener's Workbench

Rabbit Tray

Materials:
- Wooden tray
- Acrylic paints
- Brushes
- Acrylic sealer

How **T**o:

Paint the inside of the tray a base color such as the turquoise shown. Mark a center box for the central design. Sketch a design and then paint with acrylic paints. Paint a thin checkerboard frame around the box.

Paint large oval flowers all over the remaining background. Add leaves and paint splashes here and there. A wavy line adds an informal border.

Seal with acrylic sealer or have a glass insert cut to drop over the painted interior.

Credits

Special Thanks to:

Roger and Marsha Alldis at Tancredi and Morgen in Carmel,
Vicki Jo Aslanian at Cottage Gardens By-the-Sea in Carmel, Stephanie Barken, Stephen Cade and Mick,
Courtney Cassity and Leigh Kaiser, Kathy Curroto, Drought Resistant Nursery in Carmel, Nicki Dwyer,
Laurie and Catherine Fitzpatrick, L. Gay Goessling, Billy Guidry, Marsha Hall, Jesse Hickman, John Hudson,
Dianne Josephs and Emily and Morgan, Jean Lowe, Bob Mainini and Andy Wiltse, George Marquisos,
Sherri Montgomery-Resendez, Ginger Piotter at Riviera Gardens in Union Pier, Michigan, Stephanie Raaf,
Holly Saunders, Lesley Seith, Joseph Slattery, Susan Smith, Suzy Stout, Ann Walbert,
Sally Weaver, Sonja Willman, and the Decorator Showcase House in St. Louis

Contributors:

Kate and Ken Anderson, St. Louis, Missouri; page 132
Carol Baird, Carmel, California; page 81
Claude Berkwoldt, St. Louis, Missouri; pages 129, 130
Valerie Braud-Walsh, Joie de Vie, Petoskey, Michigan; page 72
Gordon Burns and Charlie Miller, Peoria, Illinois; page 28
Stephen Cade, Pebble Beach, California; page 112
Rhonda Cassity, St. Louis, Missouri; pages 16, 29, 33, 38, 68, 81, 85, 99, 110, 111, 112, 115, 126
Church of the Wayfarer, Carmel, California; page 19
Linda and Randall Comfort, St. Louis, Missouri; pages 22, 58
Tami and John Coty, Oak Park, Illinois; pages 57, 73
Amy and John Cullinane, St. Louis, Missouri; page 73
Kathy Curotto, St. Louis, Missouri; page 80
Robert Davis, Seaside, Florida; page 60
Deborah Dolgin, St. Louis, Missouri; page 52
Jim and Gloria Dougherty, Carmel, California; pages 28, 30, 44, 53, 108
Mary Engelbreit and Phil Delano, St. Louis, Missouri; pages 12, 19, 22, 23, 26, 49, 102, 108, 118, 128, 129, 132
Gail Factor, Carmel, California; pages 13, 36, 42, 51, 98
Neil and Barbara Finbloom, St. Louis, Missouri; page 99
Delia Garcia, St. Louis, Missouri; page 46, 83

Richard Gibbs, Seaside, Florida; pages 20, 47

L. Gay Goessling, St. Louis, Missouri; page 52

Nancy Gould, Gallery Americana, Houston, Texas; pages 45, 47

Frances Grate, Pacific Grove, California; page 87

Richard and Suzy Grote, St. Louis, Missouri; pages 61, 101, 114

Jeanine Guncheon, Oak Park, Illinois; page 21

Jon Hagstrom, Carmel, California; pages 14, 66, 86

Jesse Hickman, Hank's Dad, Petoskey, Michigan; page 26

Elizabeth Higginbotham, St. Louis, Missouri; page 72

Enid and Thomas Hubbard, Carmel, California; page 111

Jacqueline Hubbard, Carmel, California; page 38

Paul Ivkovich and Frances McClafferty, St. Louis, Missouri; pages 71, 117

Dennis Kaim and Larry Kisner, St. Louis, Missouri; page 127

Diana Kathrinus, St. Louis, Missouri; page 80

Kim and Steve Kelce, Glendale, Missouri; page 54

Kelce and Pedley Garden Designs, St. Louis, Missouri; page 73

Brock Larsen, Carmel, California; page 35

Kary Lockwood and Tobias Shapiro, St. Louis, Missouri; page 115

Charlotte and Andy Lyons, Oak Park, Illinois; pages 69, 70, 71, 82, 100

Hilary Mackenzie Gardens, Carmel, California; page 51

Charlotte and Charles Manassa, Carmel, California; page 87

Linda McCarthy, Carmel, California; page 35

Gayle McCormick, Houston, Texas; pages 96, 97

Connie and John McPheeters, St. Louis, Missouri; pages 20, 62, 101

Ken Miller, St. Louis, Missouri; pages 16, 29, 33, 46, 68, 81, 83, 85, 110, 112

Jean Mitchell, Carmel, California; page 55

Mary Morgan, St. Louis, Missouri; pages 35, 86

Brenda Morrison, Carmel, California; pages 31, 68

Randy Mulchay, St. Louis, Missouri; page 80

Carol Ann Newman, Washington, Missouri; pages 126, 132

Kellie O'Brien, Hinsdale, Illinois; page 109

Mary and Tom Ott, St. Louis, Missouri; pages 32, 89

Diana Pranger, St. Louis, Missouri; page 114

Ted and Sandy Reed, Herb Haus at Round Top Inn, Round Top, Texas; page 57

Ann and Gregory Rhomberg, St. Louis, Missouri; page 100

Barrie and Peter Scardino, Houston, Texas; pages 37, 48, 52, 59, 62

Tosca and Kevin Schaberg, St. Louis, Missouri; pages 32, 44

Grace Silva, gardener, Carmel, California; pages 13, 36, 42, 51, 98

Joseph Slattery, St. Louis, Missouri; pages 22, 94, 113

Shirley and Charles Steele, Carmel, California; pages 17, 36

Suzy and Sam Stout, Hinsdale, Illinois; pages 15, 50, 78, 80, 125, 128, 130

Kurt Tape, Santa Rosa Beach, Florida; page 15

Projects: